MY LIFE STORIES
The First 50 Years

Ed Gardner

Published by Ed Gardner

Copyright ©1999, Ed Gardner. All rights reserved. This book, or parts thereof, may not be reproduced in any form without permission from the publisher.

Published by Ed Gardner

Art reprinted with permission on black and white insert with credit of Ed Gardner.

ISBN 978-0-6151-8001-4

To my wonderful wife, Betty

I love her more each day than I did the day before.

Preface

This book started on August 18, 1950, in Little Rock, Arkansas. The traffic was bumper to bumper, due to a game at War Memorial Stadium, so my Dad called his friend, Sgt. Lowell J. Singleton of the Little Rock Police Department, who dispatched a motorcycle officer to escort them to the hospital. When they arrived, Dad had to pay $300.00 before they would take Mom to delivery.

Early the next morning my brother was born at 5:55 AM. He was the baby everyone was waiting for. I was born at 6:10 AM. I was the surprise! We were five weeks premature. To keep expenses down, the doctor allowed Dad and Mom to take us home. After a few weeks, we weighed five pounds. A few months after our birth, my brother had surgery to correct a hernia. He was babied ever since.

My father was a house painter, who later became a homebuilder, then a contractor, then a general contractor. He would take both of us to work so we could clean up the debris from the houses and yards.

My Mom was a stay-at-home mother, like the majority of wives during this period. She did everything a mother did and put aside enough money to keep our family going.

My sister was older than my brother and I. She was born deaf and mute, due to the long delay during the birthing process. She is talented in handcrafts, stitching and embroidery.

My Dad's mother was at the hospital when we were born. Since I was a surprise, my Dad asked what he should name us. My grandmother said, "Name the first one Freddie and the other Eddie." An uncle told him, "Name one Pete and the other Repete." That was close.

Contents

CHAPTER 1
Snippets Of My Life

CHAPTER 2
My Invention

CHAPTER 3
My Owl

CHAPTER 4
Love At First Sight

CHAPTER 5
Poetry

CHAPTER 6
My Buddy

CHAPTER 7
The Mission

CHAPTER 8
Going To A New Planet

CHAPTER 1

Snippets Of My Life

My Adventures As Superman

I was a Superman fan when I was just a little kid. Watching him on the new black and white television was my biggest thrill.

When I was four, I would have my Mom pin a bath towel around my neck, and I would spend the rest of the day running all over our yard with my arms stretched out while making the *swooshing* noise. The closest I got to flying was when I ran up a big dirt pile and jumped over the edge. It wasn't as far or high as Superman, but almost.

My childhood stopped and my education began at age six. At school, during recess, I would put on my cape and run all over the playground, holding my arms out and making my sound.

One day I had to ride the school bus. When I got on, all I had in my hand was a neatly folded bath towel. The bus driver asked me, *"What'cha got there, kid?"* I looked him square in the eyes and said, *"My cape."* Every time he looked at me in his mirror, I could see the puzzled look on his face. Apparently, he never saw Superman or a cape.

My adventures as Superman ended in the third grade. My teacher told me the safety pin could pop open and hurt me, and I couldn't tie the towel in a knot around my neck because I might get choked if my cape caught on something, and I could hurt someone if I ran into them while running around the playground.

Thanks for all the adventures, Superman.

Goose Eggs

When I was six years old, I was in the first grade. Elementary school started my education, and was new and different to me. There were so many kids around at one time, and so much to learn.

Our teacher would teach different subjects during the day and try to keep things interesting so we wouldn't get bored.

Getting bored was not my problem. Girls! They were my problem. Especially two very cute, sweet girls who always wanted to sit by me in the reading circle.

Each of them would give me a kiss on my cheek after reading time. I really enjoyed the kisses, but did not like all the jeers from the boys in class making fun of me. Being kissed by a girl! What's so bad about that?

Our teacher usually gave us tests after our lessons, and I would always not do well. After a few tests, our teacher said to me, *"Eddie, you did not get any answers right on this test. I am giving you a big Goose Egg!"* She was smiling as she marked a BIG RED ZERO on my paper. Wow, a Goose Egg! Great!

One day, my Mom came to spend the day in my classroom to see what was going on. She even walked around and helped a few of us while our teacher was doing her paperwork.

We had some fun reading time, some drawing or coloring time, and then some work learning numbers. When our teacher finished the lesson, we had another test and I got another goose egg.

Then, our teacher called me to her desk, with my Mom standing off to one side. She had all my test papers laid out on her desk, with a big red zero on each.

My Mom asked me why I was not doing my work. I showed her my papers, and said, *"I'm doing my work, Mom. Look, I'm making goose eggs."*

It was at that instant, with the class laughing, that my childhood stopped and my education began in earnest. I learned from my Mom that if I make zeros, those great big red O's given by my smiling teacher, I am failing, and I would have to take first grade over. She was serious and I didn't want to stay another year. So, from now on, no more goose eggs for me, ever!

The best part of my first grade was the reading circle. Well, actually, the kisses from the girls, but I did become an avid reader.

In fifth grade, I won a reading contest, and I received my very first book, **<u>Black Beauty</u>**[1]. Thanks to those sweet girls, Patricia and Betsy, my teacher, and my Mom, I loved reading.

---

[1] <u>Black Beauty</u> by Anna Sewell, published November 24, 1877 by Jarrold & Sons. ISBN-13: 9780486407883.

Satchel, My Dog

Family lore says that Satchel was born the same time as my brother and I. The fact is my parents got Satchel's mom shortly after we were born, and Satchel was part of a litter when we were about two years old. He was the runt and not as cute as his brothers and sisters, so we kept him.

I owe my life to this brave, caring and faithful dog. He was the family protector, guardian of the yard and baby sitter all rolled into a black and brown fur coat with a soft black nose.

One day, when I was probably four, I was playing on a trailer parked in our yard, running from front to back to make it rock up and down. When I had enough fun, I started to climb off the tailgate. Satchel ran up and started barking, jumping and lunging at me. I climbed back into the trailer and started calling for my Mom.

As she came around to the side of the trailer, Satchel did the same thing to her. She saw movement in the grass by the tires, got a hoe, and chopped up the cottonmouth when it came toward her.

He protected me from four more snakes, many dogs, other animals and strangers during my childhood and adolescence.

He was always there for me, when I needed a friend or someone to talk to or play with. His soft nose, wet tongue and wagging tail have always been my gift from him to let me know that he loved me.

Satchel will always be with me, in my heart, no matter how old I get. He was my hero.

My Art and Humor

I have included copies of two drawings that I made during my early years. I am trying to decide if I want limited editions made.

POLAR BEAR IN A SNOWSTORM

BLACK BEAR AT NIGHT

My Discovery

I was 14 years old, living in a new community in Little Rock, Arkansas. I was adventurous and loved science, astronomy and geology.

A small creek ran through our neighborhood and most of the time it had some water in it. I liked catching crawdads from the muddy edge.

One day, I was walking barefoot along the creek bed, looking for crawdads, and slipped into the soggy mud. I stubbed my toe on something while sinking deeper into the mud.

Eventually, I freed myself without having to yell for help. I went home to get a long board from my Dad's lumber pile to dig up whatever I hit my toe on in the mud. It turned out to be a large round mud ball. I took it home and washed it under the backyard faucet.

I dropped the mud ball when I saw a big bug-like thing right by my hand, thinking it was about to bite me. At least I didn't scream like a sissy. When I regained my senses, and didn't see any movement from the "bug," I continued to wash it off.

It turned out to be a white rock of sediment that had a whole bunch of trilobites and other fossils encased all around it. I showed my Mom what I found and she let me use an old toothbrush to clean it better. She told me, *"Make sure you don't get your clothes dirty and don't use too much water."*

While it was drying, I went back to the creek to look for more rocks. I found another mud ball about the same size and took it home to clean.

Some of the fossils were about the size of my thumb and large enough to see easily. Other fossils were much larger and flatter, and had what looked like many legs on the edge of their shell. There was also some seashell shaped fossils encrusted around the rock.

I read my geology and encyclopedia books to find out what I had. I talked to Mr. Owens, my principal at Cloverdale Elementary School, who was an amateur geologist and rock hound.

He asked me to bring the rocks to school so he could look at them and talk to me about my discoveries.

He smiled when he looked at my fossils and allowed me to spend extra time in the school office so we could go over both rocks carefully. Before I returned to class, he asked if I would let him take these rocks to his geology group so they could see what I found.

After a month or two, I saw one of my rocks displayed in the office window, with my name typed on a small card. I never got those rocks back from him.

Civil Defense

Our family moved from Little Rock to our lakeside cabin at Harris Brake Lake at Perryville, Arkansas. It is close to Petit Jean Mountain State Park.

Being 16, I was looking for things to do. A friend told me about the Civil Defense training about to start in town. It was going to last for eight weeks.

My brother and I learned about detecting radiation, protecting against fallout and using the Geiger counter, forms and other equipment. We would be sending monthly reports to Little Rock.

It was like Christmas in summer time! We got two boxes each marked "U.S. Government - Civil Defense Equipment." It had our Geiger counters, pocket dosimeters, chargers, lights, posters and Civil Defense signs.

Now, it was up to my brother and me to protect Perryville from radiation contamination. Every place we went, we took our equipment, especially our yellow pocket dosimeters, and took readings of the radiation levels. At the end of each month, we mailed our report forms to the State Civil Defense office.

I am glad to report that during the two years we lived at this wonderful town, there was never an incident of radiation contamination recorded.

My First Horse Jump

When I was 17, our family lived on a farm at Cedar Creek, down the road from Buck Ridge, by Center Ridge, Arkansas, and I bought my first horse. I named him Midnight. Look out cows!

Midnight was a very tall and black, and had a black saddle with silver studs around the edges. He was independent minded and trained for cutting, which the cattle trader forgot to mention.

One summer day, I was riding Midnight along an old country dirt road, just moseying along and relaxing.

Before I knew it, there was a lunge forward, then, we were airborne, heading over the top of a barbwire fence. There was just enough time for me to grab the saddle horn and hold on for everything I was worth.

After landing, I jumped off, yelled at Midnight, and thought for sure he was grinning at me. I had no idea where we were, which direction home was and just short of being afraid. I was beginning to wonder how, or if, I would ever get back home. The idea of making him jump back over by himself crossed my mind.

After thinking about it for a while, I got back on the saddle, walked him away from the fence, turned him toward the fence, gave him time to see what was about to happen, and slapped the reins on his backside while burying my heels into his flank.

We cleared the fence and ditch, landed on the road, and I opened him up for the run of his life. "Fast" was not my word to use just then. "Scared?" Yep! That's the word.

Tracking the Tracks

Our school bus driver let my brother and me off at the dirt road that led to our house. It had been snowing during the day, so it was easy to see the tracks along the ditch and fence line. There must have been probably five small deer that had passed by. The tracks were still set in the snow and pointed toward a clump of woods close to our house.

We stood still for a while, hoping to see the deer, then ran home to get our rifles and try to track them.

I mentioned to Mom and Dad that we had seen tracks up the road. We wanted to go back and see if we could track them down, and maybe bring home some deer meat. My Dad told my brother to stay home and let me track alone.

I put on my heavy pants, coat and boots and loaded my .22 rifle. Going back to where we found the tracks, I tracked the tracks over two hours through the woods, gullies and creeks and ended up behind our barn. The tracks went bad from there, so I went back to the house.

Everyone was sitting in the living room when I returned and described in great detail all the tracking I did. I mentioned the number of tracks and how I lost them in the field behind the barn.

My Dad busted out laughing, then my Mom, and finally my brother. After catching his breath, my Dad told me that five of our baby pigs had gotten out of their pen today. Mom and Dad had rounded them up just before we got home from school.

Five baby pigs. That's how many I counted. Deer? There weren't any!

High School Graduation

May 1969. It has finally arrived after all these years. The studying, writing, memorizing and tests have ended. I made it! Graduation is now a reality.

Nemo Vista High School has been my school for more than two years since my Dad moved our family to a farm in Center Ridge, Arkansas.

Nemo Vista is a complete school system with all grades in the same location. There are separate buildings for the lunchroom, gymnasium, wood shop and library with restrooms.

The high school building has a large auditorium and stage, with small separate classrooms on one side.

Mr. Ernest "Leo" Stobaugh taught math and algebra. I still have a problem figuring out what "X" is, but I did learn, *"Pi R round, cornbread R square."* How many times have I needed to find "X" or "Pi" after graduating? Zero.

Mrs. Mabel Ward taught English. Every Friday we had to spell and define 20 words in our book. We learned to use nouns, pronouns, verbs, adverbs and structure proper sentences.

Mr. Bobby Bean was the Principal, Coach and taught Physical Education. The first day I went to the gym, he asked what I wanted to do. I told him I just wanted to shoot baskets with the guys. I went through the drills in my sock feet. After class, I mentioned that I just wanted to shoot baskets during gym class. I had been training with the basketball team.

Mrs. Bean taught typing. I never learned to type without looking at my keyboard. I memorized the text while typing fast and accurately ... using only my index fingers.

Mr. T. O. Adams was the School Superintendent. He called me out of class to his office just one time to give me a prize radio for an essay I wrote about the Co-op Electrical Plant we visited during a school trip. Whew! I was nervous when he called my name. What a relief!

On the evening of graduation, all eleven of us were in one room getting into our caps and gowns. We took pictures, signed each other's cap, reminisced about school and talked about our class trip to Rockaway Beach, Missouri, with our sponsors, Mr. and Mrs. Looney.

Larry Cole was playing the piano for the audience. **_Under the Double Eagle_** started, and we walked through the audience in single file to our chairs on the stage. Mr. Adams introduced the Class of 1969. Joe Cody, Phyllis Burk and Brenda Williams gave their speeches.

Mr. Adams returned to the podium and called my name. I stood beside him while he announced that I received the **_I Dare You_**[2] award for Qualities of Leadership. What a surprise and honor.

---

[2] I Dare You by William H. Danforth, 21st edition, October 1967. ISBN-13: 978193393126.

My First Car

After many bus trips back and forth to home during three-day passes while in the Air Force, I decided to buy a car.

I shopped around, compared features and kicked the tires before deciding on a brand-new 1972 Chevy Nova Super Sport. It was satellite blue with a white top. It had more horsepower than any car on the road.

My Dad and Mom drove me to the dealer to pick it up later that day after the cleaning and detailing.

I asked my Mom if she wanted to ride back to the base with me, and she accepted. My Dad and sister would follow us.

I am a very good and safe driver. I did not do any wild driving with my Mom as passenger, but I made it back to the base in about thirty minutes. It was a while longer before my Dad arrived.

During the drive back, my Mom did not say one word. When my Dad finally arrived, and we were looking my car over, Mom unloaded on me.

"You were going 75 on the highway! What if the tires had blown out, or you had hit some gravel or a hole in the road and lost control? What if someone had pulled out in front of you? What would you have done if a car ahead of you had broken down in the middle of the highway? What if someone on a motorcycle had a wreck and was down on the highway? You were going way too fast."

Even using the new car and tires and having my licenses since I was 16 as my defense, Mom still chewed me out!

I put on some nice looking seat covers over the ones that came with the car, added a cigarette lighter for my Dad and a nice eight-track player under the dash for my long drives. I washed and waxed this beauty every week and changed the oil every 3,000 miles and checked the tires every day.

Two years later, I pulled the store bought covers off all the seats, sprayed some air freshener around and took the car to a dealer so I could buy a family sized car. This car looked immaculate like it was just off the showroom floor.

I found a beautiful 1973 Chevy Impala Custom. The sunk-in back window, desert gold color and standard features sold me.

An elderly woman pulled in behind me when I stopped the car. She wanted my Nova for her granddaughter who was going to college. She loved the car and knew her granddaughter would love the eight-track and all the tapes. She paid me the original price I had paid when I bought it. I was VERY happy.

What's In A Name?

Before my son, Eddie, was born, I had picked a name using the first names of two close friends.

Jack Reed was a family friend going back to the early days of my father. I had always told him that if I married and had a son, I would name him Jack. He shook my hand, patted my back and thanked me.

For the middle name, I was going to use Daniel. He was my friend during my days at Little Rock Air Force Base in Arkansas. He thought it was great that I would use his name.

When the big day came, the nurse handed me "Baby Boy Gardner" and said, *"What name are you going to give him? We need to put it on his nursery card and the birth certificate."* I stammered and told her I wanted to wait for my wife to confirm the name. She told me to give her a name now and I could change it before we left the hospital. Not being able to recall anything I had planned before the birth, I said, *"Eddie Gardner, Jr. for now, and when my wife wakes up, and can remember what name we agreed on, I will change it."*

This was the wrong thing to do! Men, if you have the job of naming your baby, ALWAYS write down the name you will give your child, and keep it with you. Never rely on your memory.

My two friends got a big laugh out of my predicament. My son has lived with his name, and has told me he prefers it to Jack Daniel Gardner. What was I thinking? Things worked out good after all.

Surprise Baby!

On July 19, 1973, after the birth of my son, Eddie, a nurse brought him to the room to let me see and hold him.

He had a beautiful little face, cute nose, blue eyes, black hair and all his fingers and toes. He was so precious!

On the third day, when we were getting ready to leave the hospital, my wife was getting into a wheelchair for the trip down to the car. All the flowers are on a cart with the suitcase. We were ready to go.

A nurse handed me our bundled up baby boy. I moved the baby blanket from around his face and head. The whole room froze as I loudly asked, *"Where's our baby?"* This child had a beautiful little face, cute nose, blue eyes and RED hair!

After a quick check of the prints, another nurse came in and said, *"When you first saw your son, he had baby oil on his hair, and that makes it black."*

With three globs of baby oil, and a handful of K-Y Jelly, his hair turned black.

Footprints check, name checks, hair color, finally checks. He's ours to keep and we go home.

After a few years, his hair changed to a light brown, but I will never forget the day the nurse handed me my little red headed surprise.

A Rose By Any Other Name

I arrived at Goosebay, Labrador, Newfoundland, Canada on March 23, 1975, as a new Staff Sergeant assigned to the USAF Hospital Emergency Room on the American side of the base. Later, I was in charge of the Primary Care Clinics.

My wife and three kids arrived at the end of April. She told me that I would be a daddy, again. I was glad that we had a three-bedroom unit close to the hospital.

My youngest son was born December 1, 1975. It was a hard delivery for me. I stood by my wife's side the whole time, feeling her pain during every contraction and squeeze of her hand. After the delivery, with mother and baby resting, I realized that my stomach was in knots and I was hurting. Master Sergeant Grimshaw, my supervisor, gave me two days off to recover.

When Aaron was born, many of my Canadian friends told me, *"That's a fine **Newfie** you got there, me son."* That became his nickname.

Through the years, many people asked where he got his name. I was proud and happy to tell them the story.

He held onto the nickname, or I did, until he was in the fourth grade in Enid, Oklahoma. I still cherish the memories I have of all my American, British and Canadian friends.

My First Telescope

It was a beauty. My wife, Betty, got it for me as a birthday present. This reflector telescope had all the bells and whistles for stargazing.

On a clear night, with a full moon, I set up the telescope in our backyard. I was sighting all the points of interest in the sky, trying to be the first to discover something new in the sky.

As I turned the telescope to the moon, the brightness of the light coming into the tube almost blinded me. I was watching craters and moonscape in various areas while using the rotation dial to keep things in my sight without getting the bumpy view from the tube.

All of a sudden, something came across my field of vision. I had to refocus, but was able to track it while I was busy.

I saw the most beautiful, huge, gray, slow-moving asteroid passing between the moon and me. I watched in total excitement, amazement and delight. This opportunity had happened under the perfect conditions, and I get chills when I recall this.

I had witnessed a space traveler passing in front of the moon while I had my telescope set in the right area. This reminded me of the old saying, *"Being in the right place at the right time."*

This experience was amazing and wonderful. No wonder I love science and astronomy.

MY AIR FORCE CAREER

On December 8, 1969, I left the farm and enlisted in the Air Force as a Chaplain's Assistant. Before the swearing in ceremony, my recruiter, Technical Sergeant Thorne, asked me to change my training code to 902X0. He told me I could change it later during Basic Training.

I took my first ride on a jet plane when two other recruits and I flew to San Antonio, Texas. An officer put me in command of our group during the trip. Later, I found out that it was not my leadership skills, my intelligence, or even my good looks that I was in charge. Simply, "GA" comes before GR or GO. Oh well; Texas, here we come!

It was cold, windy and dark when we arrived from the airport by bus to the receiving terminal at Lackland Air Force Base, also known as *"The Gateway to the Air Force."* A completely new world is about to begin for me.

At 0100 hours, we arrived at our World War II barracks after eating our first military meal. Our Training Instructor for the next six weeks,

Technical Sergeant Wells, was waiting to greet each of us, in the basic military style. We spent the rest of our night filling out all the required forms and documents.

Two weeks later, our other Training Instructor, Sergeant Ira Parker, returned from leave. Things really changed then! Night and day comes to mind. Easy and hard describes the change better. My one confrontation, with the brim of his hat planted firmly into my forehead, reminded me forever to stand at attention when falling out for formation.

Our six weeks of basic training had classes in military indoctrination and history, lots of marching, running, parades, firing range, immunizations, physical training and the obstacle course. Christmas and New Year were our only days off.

Near the end of basic, we were in formation to receive individual orders for our specialty training. I get a shock when I see Medical Specialist 90230 by my name. What happened to Chaplain's Assistant? The first thing I said was, "The Air Force made a BIG mistake!"

An instructor explained how I was wrong. *"You're the mistake, and you're going to be the best medic the Air Force ever had."* What could I say but *"Yes, sir!"*

With one stripe newly sewn onto my uniforms, on January 23, 1970, a busload of us travel to Sheppard Air Force Base at Wichita Falls, Texas. After being on Night Fire Patrol in the old wooden dorms for a month, I checked with Base Personnel Office, and found out my military records disappeared after I arrived. A week later, I began 13-weeks and three days of medical training.

I moved to the new dorm when classes started. When we fell-out to the covered training area, I would look at the dark morning sky and see a bright comet. Like a hazy white line, Comet Bennett cut through the sky, completely visible from end to end from February to May. It would be visible until the sun started to rise. I felt a little lonely after it was gone as we marched to class.

The biggest challenge I received was when I met a Marine hospitalized for wounds received in Viet Nam. He was alive and encouraged everyone he met.

This man had both legs and one arm missing and was forever blind. His wife stayed in his room, and helped when she could, or when he had difficulty doing something. His will and spirit was sincere and inspirational.

He told me that he was alive, his wife still loved him, and he could deal with each problem as they came up. Together, he would get through his problems and be stronger.

I have had these two in my thoughts and prayers since I met them. I hope both of you have had a wonderful life.

On May 15, 1970, I received orders for Wilford Hall Medical Center at Lackland Air Force Base. This is the largest medical facility in the Air Force.

My medical career began on June 1, 1970, when I arrived on the A-5 Medical Surgical Ward. Technical Sergeant Quentin Vaughn was my supervisor and started my training immediately. While intently watching my first medical procedure, I passed out because I forgot to breathe.

I asked him, *"How am I ever going to learn everything about the medical field?*" He told me, "*You see one, do one, and teach one.*" Many times he would tell me, "*Son, that's 9-level thinking!*" when I suggested ways to help a patient.

On August 1, 1970, during Commander's Call at the hospital auditorium, I received my Airman First Class stripes. A few days later, I was busy with patient care on the open ward area, and the volunteer kept walking around looking at my rank and saying, "*No, not you.*" I finally asked her who she was looking for. She said, "*Sergeant Vaughn told me to find the medic with one *stripe who works on this ward."* He had not received my official promotion orders. When I found him, he patted my back as we laughed about looking for me.

I have always credited TSgt. Vaughn, with his one-on-one hands-on training, for my success as a medical technician, supervisor and nurse.

To improve my medical skills and knowledge, I went to other departments after work or on my days off. My favorite was the Emergency Room, where I learned suturing, and ambulance section, going on the "lights and siren" runs.

In January 1971, against my will, kicking and screaming, I received orders to transfer to Little Rock Air Force Base in Jacksonville, Arkansas. This started with my twin brother, Freddie.

He joined about ten months after me. Three days into basic, he enters the hospital with jaundice, later diagnosed as due to a blocked gallbladder duct. After surgery and recovering for two months, where I taught him everything about being a medic, he returned to basic with specific medical restrictions, and graduated six weeks later.

He was able to change his training specialty from Aircraft Camouflage Painter, going to Nellis Air Force Base, Nevada, to Medical Trainee with an assignment to Little Rock Air Force Base, Arkansas. While there, my brother wrote our senators and used the regulations to get me reassigned to be with him since we were twins and not in a war zone.

With my 5-level Medical Specialist training, I reported for duty to the Emergency Room on June 23, 1971. I easily recertified for ambulance driving, suturing and minor surgery.

On January 1, 1972, I became a Sergeant and a shift leader.

After three years, on March 1, 1975, I sewed on my Staff Sergeant stripes. Three weeks later, I was flying to Canada on my first overseas assignment.

I arrived at the Goose Bay Airport in Newfoundland, Labrador, Canada late at night. While I waited for the other passengers to get off, the hospital "welcoming committee" came on board to "greet" me and make sure I got off the plane. I spent my first night at the "cave" at the Airman's Dorm eating cold pizza.

I started in the Emergency Room, and three months later became the Non-Commissioned Officer in Charge (NCOIC) of the Specialty Clinics. Master Sergeant Jim Grimshaw was the Superintendent of Clinics. He was the first high-ranking NCO I met who liked polishing floors more than doing paperwork. I was the luckiest person in the world to get this assignment.

We provided medical coverage from our 4x4 ambulance for firefighters battling a large forest fire near the base. We watched the water bombers fight the fire.

By the end of March 1976, after having a five-year controlled tour canceled, I arrived back at Little Rock Air Force Base, kicking and screaming, *again*.

This time, I was the NCOIC of Primary Care Clinics. Mrs. Gloria Evans was a civilian Registered Nurse who helped me improve my nursing and management skills.

About a year later, I became my brother's supervisor. This was a bad idea, and I was against it from the start, but it happened anyway. Running the clinics was a piece of cake. Getting my brother to do any work without running home complaining to our parents, and having my Dad pay a "visit" to tell me, *"He's blood and you should give him a break because you're his supervisor"* was the hard part. It was so much easier when he was working his shifts on the ward and I was in charge of the clinics.

I caught a break when Freddie decided to leave the Air Force after spending all eight years on The Rock. His wife told him that he was not going on any overseas tours alone, and she was not going to move and leave her parents.

On July 4, 1978, I drove across the American-Canadian border in Montana on my way to the Al-Can Highway, heading to Elmendorf Air Force Base in Anchorage, Alaska. The sights and scenery were fantastic and the parks I camped at were beautiful. I met many Canadian Mounties, who do not regularly wear the red coats and flat-brimmed hats, and other travelers during this trip. It stayed light into the early morning.

I arrived July 15, and reported to the Intensive Care Unit. After a year, I moved to the Emergency Room.

I received a promotion to Technical Sergeant on February 1, 1980. A few months later, I became NCOIC of Surgery Department.

The highlights of this tour are when the Hospital Commander picked me to work with a doctor to be the medical team for President Carter's fishing trip in 1980. I still have the designation pin given to me by the Secret Service agent in charge of our team.

Then, one evening, before the President's visit, I arrived at the ER and noticed a red phone sitting on the work desk. Since our crash phones were usually hanging on a wall, I thought one was broke. I failed to see "WHITE HOUSE" printed across the handle.

When I lifted the receiver to do a phone check, I heard, *"White House direct line, who are you trying to reach?"* All I could say was, *"White House? Sorry, I picked up the wrong phone. It won't happen again!"* I hung up quickly.

A short time later, two men in dark suits arrived to "discuss" the red phone with my supervisor, the Emergency Room staff and me. By the time I went to dinner, all my friends were asking, *"Have you talked to the President lately?" "How's the President?" "Did the President ask you for any advice?"*

On August 18, 1982, I arrived at the USAF Clinic at Vance Air Force Base in Enid, Oklahoma, as the Superintendent of Clinics and NCOIC of Physiological Training.

I see my past before me now. After 12 years of working in the medical field, and applying for a Physiological Training position while at Sheppard Air Force Base, I am now in charge of all this. The personnel, facility, equipment and budget are my responsibility. I can feel the weight of my past conversations with TSgt. Vaughn.

When a friend called me from Randolph Air Force Base, I mentioned that I am filling a Senior Master Sergeant position. He said, *"If you were not qualified for this position they would not have picked you."*

Thinking back to how well TSgt. Vaughn taught me, patiently and caringly, so that I could someday fill a big position, I am very grateful to him.

With the help and guidance of Captain (Doctor) Jane Curtis, a Minor Surgery Clinic opened and all the clinical equipment upgraded.

On January 1, 1990, I retired after 20 years of service, one major war, five promotions, six Permanent Change of Station (PCS) moves and one Air Force Commendation decoration.

Arriving with my family at the clinic for the retirement ceremony and party surprised everyone that forgot the date. The cake, mints, soda and memento arrived quickly and everyone had fun.

I gave my last salute to my stepson, David Russell, who was in his Air Force ROTC uniform from the University of Oklahoma.

In May 1996, he graduated from Oklahoma State University and enlisted in the Oklahoma Army National Guard.

MY TWIN BROTHER

I will mention a few examples that are different about my older twin brother and me. If he wants to give more information, I challenge him to follow me, as he always has, and write his own book.

We grew up hearing our parents tell us, *"Share everything fair and square"* and *"Share and share alike."*

When I was 13, my Dad and I had a motorcycle accident when a car hit us from behind. After recovering, the other insurance company settled with me. It was a lot of money for a kid.

While at the bank to set up my savings account, Dad said, *"Eddie, you are going to split that money with Freddie because he deserves half."* Mr. Johnston, our banker, looked surprised and said, *"Haywood, Eddie went through some pain and suffering after the accident. Freddie did not. Eddie deserves every penny he received."* My Dad said, *"That means Eddie would have more money than Freddie, and that's not fair."* My Dad ended up giving Freddie money to match my savings account that he couldn't touch until he was 21.

When we were 16, our parents allowed us to get our drivers license. On the big day, Mom drove us from Perryville, Arkansas, to the State Police Headquarters in Little Rock for the tests. We had the drivers' manual, which the officer who sent the motorcycle escort for our big arrival had autographed.

We took the written test and waited for our scores. Soon, an officer came over and called my name. I did all the car checks and showed the officer I knew my hand signals. Then we went for my big driving test.

It was a challenge in the VW Beetle, but I got through everything in one piece. The hardest part was getting the Bug up that steep hill on the way back to the test station. The officer handed me my card to get my license. <u>I passed!</u>

Freddie was not as lucky. The officer said, *"You should study the manual harder and come back in 30 days."* Mom said, *"If Freddie isn't getting his licenses, you're not getting yours either."* The officer said, *"Ma'am, you shouldn't punish him because his brother failed the test."* I got my license!

We came back 30 days later. Freddie had to start from scratch. No luck this time either. He had to study harder and come back 30 days later. After another 30 days -- same thing. Failure.

Freddie did not get his license until he was 22, while in the Air Force and after he had bought a Buick Skylark because he wanted a car like my Nova. Before he could pick up the car, we went to the Jacksonville Police Department for a driving test to get his license. He took the test, and passed, then drove my car around the station. He got his license.

OKLAHOMA CITY BOMBING

Wednesday, 9:02 AM, April 19, 1995, Oklahoma City, Oklahoma, Alfred P. Murrah Federal building. This is one of those days of history that is a part of the question, "Do you remember where you were when . . . ?"

On that day in Edmond, I was standing in front of the large mirror getting ready to shave before I went to work. The explosion rattled the mirror so hard that I moved to the hallway, thinking it was going to shatter. The sound was like a large bomb dropped on a target or an oil well storage unit hit by lightning. I called my wife, Betty, who was an Executive Secretary at the Oklahoma Army National Guard Headquarters in Oklahoma City and asked her if she had heard an explosion or felt their building shake. She had not noticed anything.

After we hung up, I turned on the television to check the local news. They broke in on regular programming with a helicopter view showing the back of the Murrah Federal building. The pilot flew to the front and we saw the destruction, with the front completely gone.

I quickly got ready for work, loaded my emergency medical pack into the trunk of my car and drove to work. No one at work was aware of the explosion, so we moved the conference room television to the break room for the news. As employees found out what happened, requests got around about making blood donations.

A doctor called me and asked if I would go to a hospital to work with the casualties with him. My supervisor declined my request, and the doctor went by himself.

After work, Betty and I drove to Oklahoma City to volunteer wherever we could help. The police would not allow bystanders to get close to the area.

After work the next day, we drove back to Oklahoma City and parked as close to the site as we could get. We noticed that boxes of supplies requested for the firefighters were piling up on the sidewalks. I started sorting the boxes and Betty asked if anyone had a truck. No one in our group had a truck, so a man walked to the street and stopped the driver of an El Camino. The owner drove away but came back minutes later and let us load his truck. People formed a line to the sidewalk and passed boxes to others that loaded them onto the trucks. The more we loaded, the more people brought boxes of supplies. Each truck took the supplies to an entry control point close to the Command Area. This continued most of the night.

Betty and I walked to the fenced area overlooking the Command Center. I noticed a firefighter leaning against the fence and bending forward. I walked to him and asked if he heeded help.

Bill Sicard introduced himself and talked to me about how exhausting his work had been, but he was OK. He was from Saint Paul Park, Minnesota and had flown down Thursday, with all his bunker gear, on a Northwest flight. He wanted to help his brother firefighters during their time of need. He was working inside the destroyed structure, removing debris using 5-gallon plastic buckets, wanting very much to find survivors. At night, he slept on a cot in the parking garage at the bombsite, quartered with the Search and Rescue team from Phoenix, Arizona.

During his three days, he had done his best and given Oklahoma everything he had. Then, on Saturday, when he could do no more, he returned to Minnesota.

On the one-year anniversary of the bombing, Bill Sicard returned for the memorial service. During his stay, he went to Mustang Elementary School to visit the class that had written him letters and made posters about the bombing. The Principal called for an assembly to the gymnasium so the students could meet and talk to Bill.

At the assembly, Bill received a Certificate of Appreciation signed by Governor Frank Keeting for his support.

Later, at the Memorial Fence, he left a plaque he made with a pair of work gloves attached and his words: *"I searched with all my heart to find someone, but I found no one, and for this, I am sorry."*

While presenting the evening news from Oklahoma City, anchor Peter Jennings ended his program reading the words and showing the plaque.

Bill Sicard returned for the fifth year anniversary, with the memorial site completed and dedicated as a national monument.

MY COLLEGE DAYS

My life story would not be complete without mentioning my college days. You have to understand that my college time extends from 1969, when I enlisted in the Air Force, to my graduation from the University of Oklahoma in 2000.

I have been a 31-year degree student, but the important thing to remember is that I completed my goal of getting a degree before I was 50 years old. Everyone should set a goal to get a college degree, because it is challenging, exciting, and a life changing experience.

I would like to use this section of my book to thank these professors for all their help, guidance, and understanding during my courses at OU.

Dr. Susan Smith-Nash has a way that makes something that sounds like a big bore into something great. Who knew Bach, Chopin, Vivaldi, Rembrandt and others had such great music!

Reading novels and books about different subjects and life experiences can make learning fun. Anyone who watched the Lone Ranger shows can recite the tune as he gallops away with Tonto. Can you remember the title of that tune? If you had Dr. Nash as your professor, you would have a great time learning that it is the William Tell Overture. She teaches you to learn from what you experience.

This book started with her encouragement and help. Thank you for letting me have a lot of fun. If I had known Humanities was this much fun, I would have taken it first.

One class that was outstanding and changed my attitude toward music was *Jazz in Japan*, taught by Dr. Sidney Brown and Dr. Joe Whitecotton.

Before this class, I only liked to listen to Glen Miller tunes. Taking this class, I learned to appreciate all jazz music, from reggae to ballroom. Listening to Dr. Brown reminiscing about the little details of the musicians and their lives was fascinating.

Dr. Joe Whitecotton accentuated the jazz class with his vast knowledge and experience as a musician. He played a great trumpet, and his band brought the old songs to life at the Border's bookstore. Who would have thought that listening to jazz and music could be so enjoyable?

Dr. Jane Bowerman helped put all my studies into something that was easy to understand and use. Her guidance and communication about any subject helped break down the confusion and gave me many "Ah-ha" moments.

Although this book is my autobiography, I added Chapter 8 as a bonus, to show what happens when groups of people work together for the benefit of a community. I dedicate this chapter to her.

CHAPTER 2

My Invention

I know that many of you who read this story will doubt it, but this is the truth. I invented the skateboard.

I was an avid comic book nut, and read all the science fiction I could buy. One of my favorites was the Marvel comic, *Fantastic 4*, and the Fantasticar. I credit my dream invention on a comic book idea.

When I was 12, I lived in a new community in Little Rock, Arkansas. There were trees all around and new blacktopped roads with a steep hill at the entrance of our neighborhood.

One day I was playing with some scrap lumber from one of my Dad's construction jobs. I had a three-foot piece of 2x10 lumber and some triangle scrap pieces that were cutouts from steps. I nailed a triangle onto each side of the 2x10 and had a long board with angled sides, like wings.

I sat on the grass in the backyard pretending I was flying the plane and fighting villains. I played for several hours without bothering anyone. Then it hit me -- if this had wheels, I could move around.

Taking my metal sidewalk skates from my closet, I flattened the sides and nailed one skate on the front and the other skate on the back of the board with wings. I reasoned that since the skates now had flat rims, I could not skate with them anymore. Now I had something that looked like it could really make good speed and it was sturdy, too. This was my Fantasticar!

I took my Fantasticar to the top of the hill at the entrance of our neighborhood for a test run. Being an overly cautious kid, I had some neighborhood friends watch for traffic. My Mom has always told me, *"Never play in the street when there are cars around, because you will get hit."* No one ever warned me about -- ROSE BUSHES!

I sat down on my Fantasticar, holding it in place with my hands on the street. After my friends knew the street was clear of cars driving through the neighborhood, I got the go ahead.

I was off! Slowly at first, enough that I had to push with my hands. Then, I went over the edge of the hill. My speed increased. I was going faster! And faster!

I was just a few feet down the hill and everything around me was a blur. I leaned my right wing down to stay in the middle of the street. I was turning right. As I was nearing the curve in the street, I leaned my left wing down. I was turning! I leaned a little more. I turned a little more!

I saw the bridge coming up quickly in front of me. Then, I remembered the one thing about the bridge that I forgot on the way up the hill. The road had a small dip before it connected to the bridge. I thought I was a goner!

I was in luck. I got over the bridge with only a hard jolt before I got the stupid idea to bail off my plane. I kept on going and was still moving fast.

I was making the hard left turn now, getting closer to my house. It was the house with the concrete driveway built to the level of the street with the rose bushes by the front porch and the big oak tree in the middle of the yard.

I banked hard left! Just not hard enough, as I sped onto the yard and into my mother's rose bushes without alerting anyone in the house!

My body has scratches and bruises and the bushes are devouring me. I left a track in the yard a bloodhound with a head cold could follow.

I had to get out of the bushes without tearing myself to shreds. Luckily, again, my friends were there to help. They had finally caught up with my travel, and were trying to pull me from the ravenous bushes.

My mother heard all the commotion outside and came out to the front porch. She looked around and was not very happy. She caught me!

Everyone heard her as she yelled *"Eddie, what in the world are you doing tearing up my rose bushes? And what happened to the yard?"*

After a whipping from my Dad for ruining my skates, and three days of having to stay inside, I finally saw daylight again.

While in confinement, I had figured it all out. Sitting on my plane was all wrong, because it did not allow me to steer well since I had to keep my hands on the wings to hold on. Standing was the answer!

Same Fantasticar, same hill, same friends, different day. Everything was ready. I started in a crouched position so I wouldn't fall too far. Then, a friend got the idea to come up from behind and give me a push to get me over the edge of the hill.

Talk about fast! I didn't have time to worry about the bridge or making any turns. I was able to stay standing on the way down the hill and it seemed like I was going a lot faster than before.

Then I remembered -- the ROSE BUSHES!

Luckily, I was able to perform the most spectacular left wing grind ever seen. I missed the bushes by a long shot. It was the big oak tree that stopped my plane.

Actually, the low brick pit around the oak tree stopped my plane. It was the big oak tree that stopped me! Being young, I easily bounced off it.

Did I mention the brick pit around the tree? Did I mention the big oak tree in the middle of our yard? Did I mention the tracks in the yard? Why is everyone staring at me? Wow! Look at the stars.

After another three days inside, and a whipping from my Dad, I thought I would never fly -- or sit. Now, I was outside again.

One of my friends asked if they could ride on my board. What a great idea! They ride; I follow. No more getting whipped -- until my mother came out to clean a friend's arm after he fell off the board. At least I wasn't grounded for another three days.

A few days later, my Dad walked over and asked me what I was doing to keep getting in so much trouble.

I showed him my Fantasticar, and got a brilliant idea. My Dad had a motorcycle! I asked him if I could tie a rope onto the cycle and have him tow me slowly down the road. After he thought it over, he started his cycle and drove it to the street. I tied the rope to the seat brace, and he drove forward slowly.

IT WORKED!

I was "skiing" behind the cycle, moving side to side by dipping the wings. This was great! I was grinning from ear to ear. We went the length of the road and back without having problems.

My friends saw what I was doing and they wanted to ride, too. My Dad was laughing from all their excitement. He asked one of my friends why they wanted to ride this thing. She answered, *"So we can go fast."* It was a complete hit.

I learned to ride standing up, and never fell while flying down the hill. We had to stop using the cycle because the slow speed burned out the clutch, so we used a bicycle. Our speed was easier to control, too and everyone took turns riding and pedaling.

I lived in the neighborhood for two more years. When we moved, it was to a lake area with no paved roads. I had to give up my Fantasticar, but I never forgot my first ride.

CHAPTER 3

My Owl

I was driving my van late one evening in Cabot, Arkansas. This heavily wooded area abounds with a variety of wildlife. I was going to dinner with my family.

Suddenly, there was a loud thud and I felt the van shudder a little. I thought I had hit something on the road, so I quickly stopped on the shoulder of the road and got out to look around. I noticed a large bloody area on the passenger door.

I looked back down the road and saw something moving around slowly on the road. I walked back and saw that it was an injured owl. I could also see that we were about to be hit by a car speeding toward us if I didn't move quickly. I grabbed the owl and jumped to the side of the road as an elderly woman sped past me while laying on the car horn.

The owl was starting to move a little while I was holding him and I worried that it was trying to get its head into a biting position. I kept its head covered between my arm and chest hoping it wouldn't get violent. I went to the van and showed them what hit us. I put him in the van closet for safekeeping.

After having dinner, we went straight home. I looked into the closet to check on the owl. This time, he was not too happy to see me, and tried to flap his wings to get out. The closet was small and prevented him from getting a good leap at me. I closed the door and went inside my house.

I found an extra-large cardboard box and some screen wire in the storeroom. I opened one flap of the box and put the screen across it. This would allow me to open the flap and see inside without letting the owl out. I found a thick branch in the yard, and after cutting a hole in each side of the box, I pushed it through the holes. This would give the owl a big perch to rest on. I cut a flap in the side of the box just big enough to get my hand through for his feeding times.

I worried about how to move the owl to the box, since I didn't want to hurt him, and I sure didn't want him hurting me. My brother took care of the problem for me. He arrived to see the owl, and I explained what I wanted to do. He put on my thick coat and gloves then put his arms into the closet to get the owl.

All of a sudden, I heard him screaming, *"He's got me! He's got me! Get him off! Get him off!"* He pulled his arm out of the closet and the owl was hanging upside down with his talons sunk into the coat sleeve and his beak open. The owl was going for my brother's hand, so I quickly moved my hand to the owl's head to keep it still.

As I moved my fingers around his head, I realized I was squeezing, but the head was still moving. The more I squeezed the deeper my fingers went into the owl's head. When my fingers stopped squeezing, I saw that this owl had a very tiny skull, but his round head was from all his soft, fluffy feathers.

I felt his injured wing, and the owl stopped moving. He must have sensed that I wasn't going to hurt him. I can't say the same about my brother. He was fidgeting around, but at least he stopped screaming.

After I got the front flap open, we placed the owl onto his new perch. He loosened his talons from his arm perch and stepped onto the limb. My brother went home whimpering and mumbling.

In the light, I could see that the owl's ruffled left wing was bloody, but not anything serious. He let me take a rag to his wing to wipe the blood off. I was probably more nervous than he was. I put an old towel in the bottom to give him something soft to stand on.

I called a local vet and found out everything I could about owls. The first thing I learned was that keeping one captive was illegal; but that's my secret. I found out I should feed the owl beef hearts and chicken gizzards, and have plenty of fresh water available. A meat cutter at a local store provided me with the hearts and gizzard without cost. This owl was going to eat like royalty while he was with me.

The next morning, as I was getting ready for work, I heard the strangest trilling sound, but could not figure where it was coming from. As I walked into the kitchen, I heard the sound from the box. It was the owl talking to me. I lifted the screened flap to look at him. "Hootie" gave me a good morning greeting as I watched him. It was the most beautiful sound I had ever heard from an animal.

When I got home that evening, Hootie greeted me with more calls. I had stopped by the library to find some books on owls to research what type owl he was. He turned out to be a barred owl, and was a very handsome bird.

I changed the water in his bowl, and got some beef heart and chicken gizzard ready to feed him. Wanting to keep him calm, I talked to him while I prepared his food. He watched my every move. Not wanting to lose any fingers, I found some long tweezers in a drawer. Hootie ate very well and walked around on his branch.

I moved his box into the living room so I could watch TV and keep an eye on him. I raised the flap that covered the screen and he seemed to enjoy the movement on the television. After a while, he called to me again, so I fed him more food. That must have been what he wanted since he gobbled everything down quickly. It was amazing to watch him.

The next morning, Hootie made the same calls as the day before. It sounded like a trilling noise, not the hoot sound everyone thinks of with owls. I fed and watered him before going to work.

That evening, I put my gloved hand inside the box, trying to touch Hootie's wing to see how it was. Cautiously, he let me examine his wing without moving. He knew his talons could tear me apart, but I was there to help him get better. There was no blood, so it was better today. I changed his water and fed him again.

He is such a handsome owl and well behaved. At night, he slept without making a sound. I could see that he was moving around on his perch each day. His health was improving each day and I know he will be going home soon.

After nursing Hootie for a month, I decided it was time to take him back where I found him. I put his box in the front seat and opened the screened flap so he could see where we were going. He seemed to enjoy the ride because he didn't make a sound.

I found the spot where we first met, and waited for all the cars to go by before I took his box out of the van. He stood still on his perch while I carried his box. I walked down a small slope toward the woods that was away from the road. I put the box down and opened the flaps.

Instantly, I heard a scraping noise of Hootie's wings against the box as he left. Then I saw his long wingspan open and heard a whoosh as he flew to the trees.

He circled the area three times, and landed on an old branch facing me. I told him, *"I'm going to miss you, but you're always welcome to come back for a visit."*

He stood up on the branch, spread his wings apart, gave me a trilling hoot and flew into the woods. Whenever I hear the sound of an owl, I always think of Hootie.

CHAPTER 4

Love At First Sight

It has been almost three years since my divorce, but I had to go back to court again to fight to continue my custody of my two sons, Eddie and Aaron. More hassle from my ex-wife. I wanted them dressed up in new clothes for the big day.

I had gone to the Enid K-Mart and found some nice dress pants, shirt, and tie for my youngest son, Aaron. Eddie wanted a three-piece pinstriped suit.

I was leaving the K-Mart parking lot, trying to make the traffic light so I could get to the Wal-Mart store down the street.

For some reason, a thought, an urge or a premonition, I didn't turn right at the light, but went straight across to J.C. Penney's at the Oakwood Mall in Enid.

While walking in, I told Eddie, *"Don't go nuts over the most expensive suit you can find. If we find one you like, I want to make sure I can afford it."*

Finding the Boys Department, Eddie found a three-piece pinstriped suit that was his size and reasonably priced. He went to the fitting room to try it on. To my surprise, the suit fit nicely and he looked sharp.

I was down on my knees, fixing his pants' cuffs, when I heard an angelic voice over my right shoulder say, *"He looks handsome in that suit."* Without looking up, I said, *"Not bad for a single parent."* As I turned to respond, the angel said, *"From one single parent to another, you did well."*

In front of me stood this beautiful blonde angel, with a voice like music, a smile bright as the sun and hair like gold. I can't remember a word we said after that. I walked around the store with her, buying things I can't remember for Eddie.

I bought the suit, and as we were leaving, Aaron said, *"That lady was really nice to us."* I replied, *"I would like to take her to lunch or dinner some time."*

He turned and ran back to this angel and, at the top of his voice, told her, *"My dad would like to take you to lunch."* She said, *"If your dad was brave enough to ask me himself, I just might go!"*

He was running back, telling me, and everyone within the sound of his voice, about me being brave enough to ask her, so I went back and asked her if she would have lunch with us today.

She agreed and then told me her name was Betty. I told her I would come back at noon to pick her up for lunch.

Our first lunch together was at Grandy's at Oakwood Mall. All four of us sat in a round booth and ordered the chicken fried steak dinner and sweet tea.

The first thing Betty did was show me pictures of her three kids, Jamie, Becky, and David. She was very proud of them.

My boys and I enjoyed the lunch with her, and I enjoyed talking with her about everything we could think of.

During her one-hour lunch, I couldn't help but look at her face and eyes. Her smile was breathtaking, and her eyes were pools of chocolate. I kept thinking to myself, *"She is so friendly, caring and family oriented. I wish I could marry her."*

Through the following months, we become better acquainted and after a year, decide to get married. We had our wedding at my parent's home in Benton, Arkansas on August 31, 1986. Our honeymoon was in the Rita Marie, an old Victorian house at Eureka Springs.

Each day has been a honeymoon, and I look forward to waking up each day so I can spend my time with her.

My favorite saying is, *"I was looking for clothes for my kids, and a wife for me, and I found both at J.C. Penney's."*

CHAPTER 5

My Poetry

My Angel

When I look into your eyes,
I see the stars from Heaven,
I hear the melody of symphonies,
I feel the air stand still,
I smell the sweet fragrance of roses

When I touch your hand,
I see the pure snow,
I hear the rapid pounding of my heart,
I feel the tender caress of a baby's skin,
I smell your special perfume.

When I speak your name,
I see lights brightly lit,
I hear the sweet song of a bird,
I feel the ground shake and rumble,
I smell the cool air as it surrounds you,

When you are with me,
I know Heaven is near,
Because I am with an angel.

By Ed Gardner, 1999

CHAPTER 6

My Buddy

Derek is my grandson, who was born in Enid, Oklahoma three weeks after I married Betty.

One night, we got the call from Jamie that she and her husband were going to the hospital for the delivery. We raced to meet them.

When we arrived on the maternity ward, we went to the waiting room with the other family members. About 45-minutes later, I hear a baby crying and said, *"That's my grandson crying."* They dismiss me as being a wishful Grandpa since there are other babies on this ward.

Just a few minutes later, the nurse arrived and told us we can visit mother and baby. I told the nurse that I heard a baby crying. She said, *"That was him you heard. He's the only boy baby we have on the ward tonight, and the only boy born this week."* They gave me a large metal button to wear that read **"IT'S A GRANDSON!"** What a cutie pie. He's just a little precious bundle of sweetness.

When Derek was three months old, he contracted one of the worst cases of bacterial meningitis treated by the local doctors.

The first spinal tap culture showed three layers of bacteria growing within a few hours of incubation. His only hope was a new and powerful antibiotic. Our concern was if it would work in time to save his life.

While Derek lay unconscious in his crib from the swelling around his brain, connected to IVs in his scalp, arms and ankles, and monitors recording his vital signs, his Mom, Grandmother (Betty) and I watched and waited. His neurological signs were slipping, and his coma grew deeper.

We could do nothing except watch the monitors. I was able to hold him in my arms, hoping to comfort him from his pain.

Many other family members had arrived and where crowded into his room. I noticed a change in his heartbeats on the monitor, and started to watch it closely. No one else was aware of the change.

Then it happened. I saw his precious little hand quiver, and the monitor go into the start of a saw-tooth pattern. I put him back into his crib and rang for the nurse.

Just as she entered the room, his monitor went flat line. She ran back to call a "code" while I cleared the room.

I was able to gently and calmly move everyone into a waiting room across the hall. I told Betty, *"Derek is dying, and they are calling a "code" to resuscitate him. The doctor will be here very soon."* Dr. Meyers, a Flight Medicine doctor I worked with at Vance Air Force Base Clinic, arrived quickly and started the procedure for resuscitation. The nursing staff worked as a team using their training to keep Derek alive.

Some people would say it was the doctor and staff fighting for Derek's life. Others would say it was the medicine that worked to kill the infection. I would say that God performed a miracle in that room. What I saw gave me hope.

While the doctor and nurses were doing their work, Derek held his little arm up in the air. I knew then that his brain, at least for that brief time, gave him the power of movement.

As the days went by, the antibiotic continued to work and we could see Derek responding in very small ways.

Each time the doctor wanted to perform a spinal tap, he permitted me to assist. I would hold Derek in the required position, and whisper in his ear, *"Derek, Grandpa loves you. Be still and don't move. We'll be done in a while."* I wanted to help in any small way and let him to know that I was there for him.

All the doctors kept telling us that, if Derek survived, we could expect multiple health problems such as possible deafness, blindness, retardation, mobility problems, breathing difficulty or all these. There was no way to know yet.

Three weeks later, Derek was looking around, raising his arms and kicking his legs. It was wonderful to see.

After all these years, the precious sights have continued. I have watched him learn to read, swim, run, ride a bike, play baseball, basketball, football, street hockey and just be a kid.

When he was seven years old, we took him on a trip to Estes Park, Colorado. Along the way, he read the signs posted on the side of the road, counted the big trucks we passed, and asked if we were there yet.

When we went swimming at the hotel pool, Derek hesitated to jump into the pool, so I stood in the water and told him I would catch him. He jumped into my arms, and then splashed around, with me holding him. He wanted to do it again, and again, and again. We had lots of fun. He lost his fear of water.

To me, though, the most precious words I love to hear from him are, *"Grandpa, I love you."*

You are about to read my two bonus books I have included in my autobiography. The first story is about the encounters of an enlisted serviceman on a dangerous mission. The second story tells of a group of people traveling to another planet.

This book has been exciting, fun and challenging for me, and I am looking forward to my next book about the decade after my book completion. Enjoy!

CHAPTER 7

The Mission

With time, military service can turn a boy into a man. A battle for your life will do it in a hurry.

I was on a classified mission in the Air Force. This was the time I felt like I was doing something - for God and Country. No one would ever know about this mission, and if I made it back, I probably wouldn't even get a medal.

With all my fears forced down to the bottom of my gut, I got ready to sleep in my sleeping bag the first night out. The mission will be hard and long, and I need all the sleep I can get.

Trouble begins when I wake suddenly, fighting to get the tent off me while I'm still inside my bag with the canvas pressing on my face. The darkness under the tent is working against me, and I can't get my bearings.

I finally get out of my bag and try to stand up with the tent still pressing down on me. I crumble to the ground, my head blazing with pain and my ears ringing. I counted the stars as I slip into unconsciousness. My world goes dark.

I hear the sound of a thousand buzz saws in my head, but I can't focus on where I am or what is happening. I can't see any light, and I can't tell if my eyes are even open. My head feels like a jackhammer is working inside. I can't draw a good breath, and when I try, my chest feels like a hot poker is being run through me.

I hear a person talking and laughing, but can't understand what they say or where the sound is coming from. I try to bring my hand to my face to wipe the sweat off. My hand doesn't move. I try to move my head up, but it doesn't move. I feel weak and disoriented.

Instantly, I freeze! My stomach does a painful flip as I realize I'm a captive about to be interrogated. My hands and feet hurt from the tight rope, a board is jammed under my arms and across my shoulders, a bag is over my head and tied tightly around my neck. They have my body in a captive position that causes me extreme pain with any movement.

I feel the first crack of the gun butt across the back of my shoulders as a person on each side yanks me to my feet. I'm an easy target.

The next hit is from a fist to my midsection. I lose my breath. I feel like I'm going to die before my wind comes back. Then, I feel the sharp pain of a switch across my thighs.

A man yelled something I couldn't make out in my ear. Then I hear a voice ask me in English, *"Who are you and what are you doing here?"* My training takes over, and I yell my name, rank, and social security number, and I ask, *"Where is 'here'?"* Thank God, I blackout as the yelling and beating starts. The pain slips away for now.

Again, I wake up. My body feels like it has been run over by a bulldozer. There isn't a part of my body that doesn't hurt. At least this time I can see a small point of light through a hole in the hood. I concentrate on it with all my effort, but everything I see is blurry.

I hear the same question again. I give the same reply, this time without asking where I am. The voice behind me laughs. He says something I can't understand, but I hear movement around me. Again, he asks me if I know where I am. I reply, *"No."* He laughs again.

He yells, *"You will only answer questions. You will not ask questions. Each time you tell a lie, you will receive the switches."* There goes my stomach again.

He screams, *"Why are you here?"* I tell him, *"I went to sleep in my own bed, and I woke up here."*

My head cracks the ground as they yank my feet into the air. The switches begin at my feet and work down toward my head. I feel my blood pouring down my body. The searing pain starts to go away as my world goes dark again.

I wake to find myself looking up from inside a small pit with wooden poles pressing me down with dirt up to my neck. My hands are free but it hurts to move my arms to my face. My whole body stings wherever I touch. My face feels like a piece of raw meat, but I have my sight.

I try to gather my thoughts and figure out how I got here. Then I hear another voice whispering to me. I whisper back asking if he can hear me. It's one of my team members on this mission. I'm not alone!

He tells me, *"They overran our camp the night our mission started. They cut the tent ropes to make it fall, shot anyone running out, and clubbed or knifed anyone still under it. They dumped our bodies in an old burial pit outside the main camp. We are probably the only survivors."*

Suddenly, I go deaf from an explosion and my body snaps into a fetal position. I let out a blood-curdling scream from the pain of my movement. The ground around me moves in all directions. I see flashes of white and yellow even with my eyes closed. I smell the musty odor from the dirt as it falls on me as I focus my energy on getting out. I hear shouts from all directions, but can't tell what they are saying.

I take hold of the wooden poles with my hands and push as hard as I can. I'm free! I crouch down in my pit, look around, and then start to slither out. As I look back, I see another shallow grave. I move to it, and see the radio operator from our team. He's buried like I was but the poles are harder to move. With him pushing as I pull, they come out.

We look around and then crawl to a crater close by. We are in luck. There's a dead man with a rifle, two belts of ammo, and a knife. I give the knife to my buddy, pull two bullets from a belt and hold them. We look at each other and nod in silent understanding. We know what we have to do if they capture us again. I put them in my shirt pocket, just in case. There's a 10-round clip in the rifle. I put the ammo belts across my shoulders.

There's lots of shooting going on around us, so we carefully look over the rim of the crater. We see a wooden tower about 40 yards away with two guards shooting in our direction, but more toward our right. They must not have seen us yet.

I sight down the gun barrel and squeeze the trigger. I don't remember hearing the report, but see one man go down. I quickly take aim on the second man and squeeze the trigger again. The shooting stops.

We run toward a truck about 50 feet from us. We crawl under it and see another tower about 40 yards away with two guards firing a machine gun to our right. Again, I sight one, then the other.

I spot six men lined up, crouching on a shack porch, firing in our direction, but more to our left. Three more are shooting from a ground pit in front of the porch. They seem to be concentrating their fire at something that we can't see. They haven't spotted us yet.

I sight the last man on the porch and squeeze. Then the next, the next, and the next. They shuffle around some as I drop the last two on the porch. I feel a click, and reload. I take aim on the men on the ground, and sight the man in back and squeeze again, and again, and again.

While we are waiting to see if the fighting is over, a man runs out the door yelling something and I drop him in his tracks.

There is an explosion and the area to our left now has a big crater that has two large trees crisscrossed and hanging over the rim. They haven't spotted us, so we run to the new crater and huddle under the fallen tree trunks and catch our breath.

I load a new clip into the gun as my partner loads more bullets into the old clip. All of a sudden, I hear a sound like giant bees buzzing around. We watch as bodies fall to the ground and convulse as dirt flies all around us. We realize that "Puff the Magic Dragon," a modified Hercules C-130 gunship, was working far above us. Moving to the crater was the best luck we've had so far. We didn't get a scratch.

After the buzzing stopped, we heard the beautiful sound of a chopper coming in, but we coudn't tell where it was. Our crater suddenly got dark, and we looked up, and smiled great big smiles. A harness came down from the chopper and my buddy got into it and quickly flew up and away. The sunlight in my eyes told me the chopper took off under fire. I looked around to see three men with rifles standing in an open area pouring fire toward the chopper. I got off three good shots and the shooting stopped.

I heard a loud noise, looked up, and saw a chopper above me just as the harness hit my head. I pulled it around me in no time, and I flew up and through the door. It happened so fast I didn't have time to be afraid of heights or flying. A crewman sat me against a wall and motioned for me to cover my eyes.

I don't remember hearing any noise, but I saw the bones of my hands and fingers that I had over my eyes. I felt the chopper shudder, but it was still moving up and away. The crewman pulled my hands down and yelled to me that it was OK to open my eyes. As I looked out the chopper door, I saw the charred and smoking landscape.

They had used four Hades bombs on this location. These bombs are BIG, and pack a lot of flammable gel that burns everything when it explodes above the ground and blows down. The explosion sucks air out of the area instantly, then it flashes into flames and heat a few seconds later. If the concussion doesn't get you, the flames or heat will. Even a pit or bunker isn't safe. What "Puff" didn't take care of, the Hades bombs did.

The crewman told me my buddy is in the other chopper and we are heading back to base. We are leaving here alive.

He tried to take the rifle from me, but I had a tight grip on it. He told me that he would get it back to me later. I finally let go of it. I saw that it was a Chinese SKS.

I felt a flood of relief come over me. It has been four days. I curled up in a corner of the chopper and fell asleep. I was happy to be going home.

Now, all I have to remember this mission is my hearing loss and bad back.

CHAPTER 8

Going To A New Planet

I cannot believe it! Today, January 1, 2018, starts a trip to a new planet. The goal is to transplant a colony of earth people to a planet somewhere in the Alpha Centauri star system. This idea started after I graduated from the University of Oklahoma in 2000.

I woke up early to make sure my personal things are in order before taking my first flight into space. Flying has never been my strong point, so I am hoping that I will be sleeping after we board the shuttle transporter.

At that time, the world was full of national and cultural conflicts, pollution, wars and population problems. Some wealthy individuals around the world decided to finance a private space mission to transport a small group of people to a new planet.

My selection was part of a four-nation program of space exploration and colonization. Dr. Jane Bowerman, my Inter-Area Studies professor, put in a very nice letter of recommendation that got the attention of the upper management.

Part of my college studies was learning about where we are going as a country and a civilization. Now, I will be able to tell her from my own personal observations about where we are as a team, our cultural makeup, how we interact with one another and all the changes that occur.

Each nation chose a member to join this mission. Each of us has a specialty that will be critical during this journey. The team members will have their spouse and family members traveling with us so that we can continue a genetic lineage.

My family will consist of my wife, her oldest daughter and her husband, their son and his wife, and their daughter and her husband. Her son and other daughter and my two sons decided to stay on Earth.

The three nations joining in this experiment are Asia, Unified Europe and Africa. The Asian and African team members each brought their wife, and both couples have three children of various ages. The European member brought his wife and a daughter with her husband and child.

Having our family and children with us reduces the anxiety of never being able to return to earth in our lifetime. It will allow for aging and the continuation of our species after we settle on the planet.

Our ship is a sphere constructed in space exactly between earth and the moon where the zero gravity played an important part in the construction. A sphere is the simplest form that has no edges or corners and the lack of gravity allowed a perfect fit during construction.

The lining of the outer shell of the sphere has hollow carbon rods manufactured by a University of Oklahoma chemist. These carbon rods are 10,000 times stronger than steel. Each rod has a fiber optic strand that gives the sphere a transparent appearance when viewed straight on because the strands transfer light from all sides. The rest of the space in the carbon rod contains a continuous strand of titanium wire the width of a hair. This is the strongest metal produced on earth.

The carbon and titanium make this ship virtually indestructible and highly maneuverable. The amazing thing about this sphere is the outer sphere encloses a smaller inner sphere built the same way.

Both spheres are separated by a thin space filled with krypton gas. This separation allows the outer sphere to spin at 12,000 miles per hour, which will generate all of our electrical needs while giving the hull an electromagnetic charge to repel space objects.

The rotation will allow us to guide our ship in any direction. The inner sphere will remain motionless with normal gravity and stability to help us maintain balance and direction in space.

The twelve solid fuel rockets will push the sphere to a speed of 180,000 miles per second, just under the speed of light. They will follow the sphere using the electromagnetic charge generated as a shield, then used as shelters at our new location.

Since we will be traveling slower than the speed of light, the trip to the Alpha Centauri system will take almost five years to complete.

I was a nurse and safety consultant before accepting this project, so I monitored health and safety issues. Since we were going to be working and living in the sphere for years, everyone agreed that health and safety would be one of our greatest concerns. We even looked at safety from the children's perspective, and had to modify our systems to protect our young, very precious future.

The day has arrived and we finally depart the airplane bringing us to our High Velocity – High Altitude (HV-HA) Transfer Vehicle launch site built at the North Pole. Launching from here will allow us to escape much of the gravity and altitude problems past launches encountered at the southern sites.

By using the transfer vehicle, the wealthy backers of this project have done away with the unsightly launch platforms used in the early 1950s.

Modern climate controls built into our clothing allow us to move around in this cold climate without worrying about the 70 below zero temperature. If we put on the helmet, we could walk around on the ice or do a spacewalk. There are no spacewalks planned during this trip, but we have trained for this, just in case.

The launch site facility is new and comfortable, but the views from the small portholes do not let us see much for our last look at earth.

My family and I met with the other expedition team members and their families. We have had meetings before, but not with everyone at the same time.

Each team member has a specific role to play in this mission, so we have taken classes to learn to speak the other languages and learn about the different cultures. The other members and their families voted that English would be the preferred language. The only difficult thing for me to learn was the change to the metric measurement system and algebra. I am the only team member who does not speak more than two languages.

The three other team members requested a separate meeting with me to decide who our leader would be. I get a surprise when each of them cast their vote for me. I only voted for myself because I knew I could do the job, but never expected the others to make it unanimous.

They told me it was due to my vast experience as a military leader, my calm demeanor in a crisis, my medical skills, my knowledge of astronomy, and my understanding and capability of working with other people, that I they selected me. They were comfortable with me as their team leader and knew that I could keep order between everyone during our mission.

After making sure our personal affairs were in order, and a quick celebration with the wealthy backers, we boarded the HV-HA vehicle that would get us to the space shuttle that is in orbit, waiting to take us to the sphere.

The supersonic takeoff was not bad since the invention of the pulsating chair that reduces G-force compression. We got to the edge of space in less than ten minutes.

It was thrilling being in the zero gravity environment again as we head to the shuttle. Then, real life takes over.

Even with all this technology, my granddaughter had a slight case of motion sickness. I put the modified electrical nerve stimulator unit on her wrists and neck, and this seemed to help keep her airsickness in check. It might have been the view of earth moving so fast that caused her reaction. The other members and I fared well. I have never liked flying since I was a kid, when I was a passenger in a small airplane.

After one hour in space, and a restful nap for my granddaughter and me, we make it to the orbiting shuttle.

The shuttle arrived ahead of us after modifications to carry the four POD (Personal Observation Device) units. We will use these to transfer over to the sphere and as our escape vehicles if we have to leave the sphere in an emergency. They are exactly like the sphere and can sustain each family for over a year.

After we float through the airlock tunnel, we settle down in our seats in the front quarter. The shuttle moves out of high earth orbit toward the sphere. After four hours, we have our first look at the sphere.

It was humongous! I see the surprise on everyone's face. The view filled our large view screen. With the moon behind it, the sphere appeared to be twice as big. When we got closer, we realized that the fiber optics effect gave the appearance of being enormous, since it was only four miles wide.

When we are within one mile, each team member and their family got into their POD in the transport bay. One at a time, we maneuver out of the cargo bay and head for the sphere. Each team finds their entrance points on the sphere and merge through the shells. After securing each POD, the entry hatches open at the same time.

Inside the sphere, we ready our assigned stations. It is comfortable and the light inside is remarkable. It is starlight and pure light to see true colors in space.

We got through our checklists, tested the equipment, found our living quarters and activated the fiber optics and communication computer. This allows us to see the moon on our left and earth on our right.

We come up with an all green board and I announce, *"The board shows all green for go, together as a team."* Everyone agrees and expresses excitement at being here.

Mission Control confirms our status and we take control from ground operations. Our destination is straight ahead.

We start the outer sphere spinning. In no time, we are generating our own power and the electromagnetic field. Our mission is finally ready to begin.

Leaving earth orbit was more anticlimactic to what we were anticipating. The four starter rockets fired and pushed us out of orbit, but we had no sensation of moving except watching the moon and earth moving away from us.

We reached 40,000 miles per second, just after Jupiter, when the other rockets kicked in. We did feel a slight change in velocity then, but we allowed the computer to control the sequences, and just sat back for the ride. We will be getting to our travel speed that we will maintain during this mission.

After an hour, our computer informed us that we had reached 180,000 miles per second. This is fast! Our view outside did not give us a feeling of great speed, but we knew we were moving, because the earth and moon are large specks on our view screen. We set the main computer program that will maintain our course, speed and communication for us automatically.

After we completed our work, we gathered for our first meeting. I explained that our mission was to travel to the Alpha Centauri star system, and start a new colony of humans. We were going to transplant humanity to another planet.

Each of us, as a team, and as a family, has the goal of reaching our new destination. We will be using the latest technology to help us accomplish what was only a dream a few years ago. Having our families will help relieve the anxiety of never going back to earth in our lifetime.

I reminded them that everyone had donated tissue samples years ago, and there is a clone of each of our organs in the medical department available for transplanting if there was a medical necessity. Everyone was happy with their situation and eager to finish the mission.

Each team member and their families will have their own section of the sphere to call home. We agreed to new customs of confinement that allowed informal boundaries. Everyone voted for my family to have the center living area since I was the leader.

I requested that my position be the commander or leader of our group and not as a political or governmental position. Everyone agreed, and since there was freedom of speech and election, I requested that only the team members work in a hierarchy of authority to reduce time completing any orders given by me. I requested that the Asian member be my second in command, then the European. The African member, being a scientist and geologist, requested not to be in a position for command, but agreed to follow all orders.

Each of us will continue to perform our specialized tasks we have trained for, but this agreement brought order. We are now a civilized community.

We agreed to have the computer keep track of our day and night cycles in the sphere. Since we were traveling close to the speed of light, a regular calendar would be almost impossible to keep. That will have to wait until we arrive at our new home planet. Now we will find out if there is such a thing as space lag on the body.

We are six months into our trip, and the computer gives an alarm about a large black hole that is near our course. Our science members review the information gathered by the computer scan.

We decide that we were not going to be in any danger or have any problems, and use the communications link with Mission Control to send our decision. Studying this phenomenon in detail is the pinnacle of our careers. NASA and other scientific organizations receive our information of this never before witnessed event.

Each member agreed that my wife and daughter should organize a school program. Much of the information gathered during our trip will enhance the standard class material.

Part of our education is learning to cope with living and working together during this trip, so we start with a humanities course. Where better to begin studying about us than at the beginning. In the years to follow, our ancestors will use this journey as a history lesson.

Later, the European member's wife, who was a geneticist, started a genetics study program. It was helpful since she is responsible for the cloned cargo on board.

With all the diversity aboard this ship, we were writing our own social, ethnic and cultural guideline as we travel.

As the days passed into a year, we were thankful to have the computer supporting our needs. We started the day with an alarm concerning an increase in radiation from a star cluster close to our path.

Using our scientific information and the computer link to NASA, we were able to reconfigure the electromagnetic field around the sphere and block all the harmful exposure.

Now, 16 months into our trip, we have the greatest event I can think of during this mission.

We have encountered a comet that closely paralleled our route. Using a POD, we got within 30 feet of the ice core and took fantastic pictures. This will help us update information gathered during the 1999 Stardust project.

Since we were able to manipulate our electromagnetic field, we caused a major gravitational pull on the comet. We are now carrying to our new home planet a piece of deep space debris that some scientists might theorize was responsible for the beginning of life on other planets, maybe even Earth.

We have been on our journey for 23 months now. We have researched Einstein's theory about aging and space travel. Each member and all the families have reviewed pictures taken when we first came on board the sphere. Each of us is as young looking as we were the first day we arrived.

With all the science and genetic research, we have concluded that Einstein's theory that traveling at the speed of light reduces time, therefore, also aging. There is no evidence found of degeneration on our bodies.

Just two days after our 30th anniversary, our sphere made direct contact with a ten-mile wide asteroid. The section of the space rock that hit the carbon and titanium hull bounced off and did not cause any damage.

The asteroid had a structure composed of multiple asteroids loosely compressed into the large formation that broke apart after the impact. Using a POD, we brought samples on board, and the rest is in tow.

Three days after the asteroid contact, the European physicist and the African geologist have found evidence that this rock hit earth thousands of years ago. After the collision, this piece continued back into deep space. From the samples gathered, we have found large amounts of gold, silver and iron in one section.

One week later, they discovered the ferns and fossilized trees in a deep pit filled with pulverized dirt, shale and frozen water. The cold space has preserved everything for us to examine.

We may have saved this mission because this rock was on a direct path to Alpha Centauri.

During our three years of travel, we have celebrated the birth of seven children. My daughter had a little girl, my grandson's wife had a little girl, the African member's oldest daughter had twin boys, and the European member's daughter had a boy and later, twin girls. They are all healthy and happy.

Today, we realized that we have not given our sphere a proper name. We have just called it the sphere as a common description. Since we have had great discoveries and births of new life onboard, we christened our sphere "The Ark."

We have been traveling over 39 months and receive a priority message from Dr. Jane Bowerman, who is celebrating her "35th" birthday today.

She informed me that since I was leader during the discovery of the fern fossils, David Boren, formerly a senator from Oklahoma, and later President of the University of Oklahoma when I graduated, now President of the United States, has granted me a Doctoral Science Degree in Deep Space Studies. This the only degree of this kind ever granted by the College of Science.

The other members and wives received a Doctorial Degree in Space Research and Planetary Exploration for their work on this mission.

After this news, we had a big, loud and happy celebration! Like all college students, we know how to study hard, party and have lots of fun.

It is our 40th month, and the Asian members' wife tells everyone at our meeting that she is two weeks pregnant. She will also give birth onboard as we get closer to the new planet. It is anyone's guess as to who will be the first to give birth to the first citizen on the new planet. We cannot wait to see how this turns out. Everyone has remained happy and healthy and our families are growing.

I thought the comet and meteor discoveries would be the highlight of this mission, but I was wrong. The Ark has really proven its strength and endurance to us this week.

On our 49th month, the main computer sensor warned us of a sun that was going supernova and was straight ahead of us. There was no way to stop or change course in time to avert a disaster.

The scientists reviewed the plans of the sphere, came up with an idea of increasing our speed by placing all our PODs on the leading edge of the electromagnetic field and match the rotation of The Ark. We should be out of danger before the supernova happens.

We get everything set up and start the experiment. In less than two minutes, we have increased our speed to 185,950 miles per second. The possibility of doing this was unknown and untested. We worked as a team and gave it our best shot and we won.

Three days after we pass the star area, it went supernova. The explosion damaged three rockets, but our electromagnetic field protected us.

We got the surprise of our life when we discovered the blast pushed our speed to 193,215 miles per second. We are traveling faster than light. This validates the Galilean space-time theory on the existence of absolute time. There is no distortion of the sphere, so it is possible to travel faster than the speed of light!

With perfect timing, the Asian member's wife goes into labor and I prepare the medical area for the delivery. This was the easiest delivery I have ever had. The baby girl was born shortly after the labor started, but the mother did not have any hard labor or difficulty delivering. I feel grateful that my training allows me to be a part of this wonderful event. All the births seem to be getting easier to deliver.

This delivery is another first for our history books, since the baby arrived while traveling faster than the speed of light. Mother and baby are doing well and enjoying their time together.

By working together as a team, we determined that using each POD and reversing the direction, we would slow to our old speed.

The pods were set in place and the outer sphere reversed directions at twice the current speed. The idea worked like a charm, and we slowed to our old speed of 180,000 miles per second. We will not overshoot our target area. What a great team we have here.

After the supernova, our detailed inspections from the PODs verified that The Ark actually deflects all radiation and debris into deep space due to its makeup and the electromagnetic field. Our interior gravity remains constant like it was on earth.

We sent our data on the supernova and traveling faster than light speed to NASA. We transmitted a message to the makers of our fiber optics package to tell them how good it has worked. Then, we sent a message with our field notes about the carbon rods to the developers at the University of Oklahoma. This will revolutionize space travel and improve the safety of future voyagers.

It takes longer to contact earth since we are farther away, but we are making history and rewriting the science books as we travel deeper into space.

We have been transmitting all of our information and receiving messages only on special occasions, as we planned before the start of this mission. Everyone, including the children, take turns estimating how long a message takes to arrive from our location to earth. This is a great mathematical brain exercise and the younger kids do very well working the calculations.

We used to get frustrated having to wait one minute for the microwave to heat coffee. Things have certainly changed since the invention of Alexander Graham Bell's telephone and Marconi's wireless telegraph.

We are nearing our destination now. It will be less than eight months before we transplant to our new planet in the Alpha Centauri system. We start our search for the suitable planet to homestead. It is hard to believe that we made the impossible very possible, and we have not had a single loss of life.

Today, we are actively searching for diseases and infections that we might have brought with us. As a precaution, we will irradiate all inanimate material before we start for the planet's surface. Everyone has developed total immunity to all viruses, and everyone has shown regenerative healing after any trauma. We believe it is because of the electromagnetic field that has improved each of our immune systems. It has been more than four years since the last recorded illness.

We have developed equipment that will determine the presence of any organisms the planet has that might be a hazard to us. If there are, we will first try to make an immunization for everyone. If that does not work, we will have to take our chances, since this is a one-way trip.

Today, with three months to go before landing, we have learned my granddaughter is expecting a baby. We now have our answer of who will be the first citizen of the new planet.

We have a party to celebrate the great news and our mission.

Since we are close to landing on the planet, we will have time to construct the shelters, organize our community, cultivate the land and explore our surroundings. The other members and I are taking bets if the baby will be a boy or a girl. I bet it's a boy!

We program the scanning computer with the environmental and scientific requirements for selecting planets capable of supporting life. After long-range scanning, the data points to the Alpha Centauri A sector as our best bet in having a successful colonization mission.

The Alpha Centauri section has three star systems that we scanned. The "A" and "B" systems are binary, and orbit around each other. The "C" system is still further away, and has its own separate orbit.

The "A" star system appears to provide better data that supports our requirements for life. The "B" system lacks many of the necessary requirements we are looking for, so it will be our second choice. Section "C" is too distant to get any firm data, so we decide it will be our last resort.

We perform a more detailed scan of section "A" to see what is available that we could call home. In a short time, we find one planet that has many of the same qualities of earth.

Unlike earth, this new planet is the forth planet from a slightly larger yellow sun and has a smaller moon. It spins on an axis comparable to earth and the speed of rotation compares to earth's 24-hour rotation. It is in the life zone of the sun and has a stable planetary orbit. An atmosphere is present, since we detect water that could be clouds or vapor.

The report shows it may have the same gravity as earth, and all the heavy elements, like oxygen, carbon, nitrogen and iron. There is nothing like having heavy elements to keep life going.

We meet with everyone and review the information we have on this planet and take a vote. We decide to go for landing on this planet, soon to be our new home, going as one group and facing the challenges together.

We will prepare for everything, and understand that if we do not make it, the end will come at the same time.

After traveling over 4.3 light years, we are within 1,000,000 miles of our goal. We continue to scan the planet for more data as we prepare to slow The Ark to prevent overshooting our target.

We decrease the rotation of the outer sphere and slow The Ark to 30,000 miles per hour. We position the rocket boosters to the front as they thaw from the deep-space hibernation for the retro fire.

Today, we are 750,000 miles from our new home. We briefly decrease the rotation of the outer sphere and the rockets leap away from The Ark.

We increase our spin and the sphere's field, and use the rockets as retro engines that fire at the same time. All the rockets press against the electromagnetic field and we slow to less than 1,850 miles per hour. We release the rockets from the field and they appear to leap away from The Ark. We increase our spin again.

With 500,000 miles to go, we are aware of our slower speed as we seem to crawl toward the planet. After two hours, the rockets contact the outer atmosphere. We watch as the final stage rockets fire and descend to the surface.

We spin up the outer sphere, and decide to maintain a synchronized orbit 1,000 miles above our new home to observe the rockets' entry and landing.

After the entry fireball, the paraglide chutes open and guidance engines maintain each rocket's projected course. Our monitor shows a final burst of the landing stage engines help make the programmed soft landing. Each rocket survives the entry and landing with all but one lying down on the ground grouped in a planned formation. The one standing will be our observation tower.

We do not see any other activity as we monitor our scanners for the next 72 hours. After studying the data, we decide to leave our synchronized orbit and scan as much of the planet as possible. This will help us learn the terrain of this planet and check for inhabitants that may already be living here in isolated areas.

After ten days of continuous scanning, we determine we must be alone on the planet. We have joked over the years about talking to the inhabitants upon our arrival. Here, we will be able to colonize this planet ourselves.

Since we came without weapons for defense, we would have been helpless if we had encountered inhabitants. That was not in our mission plan, and we would have searched for another planet.

Everyone is busy getting all the equipment and gear stored away for final entry to our new home.

We decide to modify a POD to remain in a synchronized orbit as the communication satellite after we start our entry. This POD receives two programs for our communication to earth.

The first program, if there is no signal received from us within 30 days after we descend, is for a continuous message that we have crashed and there are no survivors. We program the computer to follow our path of entry so there is no usable material or items if we do not survive the landing.

The other program is the message that we landed safely on the planet and we are beginning our colonizing mission. The POD will then provide us information, communications, weather data and early warnings of space objects.

We vote that we wait until we are safely on the planet before making any decisions about naming our new home.

The time has arrived, and we prepare for landing on our new home planet. Everyone gathers into their assigned pod, ready for the unknown.

By remote control, we start the computer control for the entry sequence after moving the message pod outside the range of The Ark's electromagnetic field. We will know in a few hours if everything goes well. If not, we hope for a quick and painless end.

As we start to descend, we feel a slight buffeting and the view screen blurs as The Ark hits the outer atmosphere. With the stabilizing computer working as great as it always has, we stay in an upright position and feel only small bumps as we go in.

The command computer informs everyone that the temperature around the electromagnetic field is over 8,000 degrees Fahrenheit. We see a yellow glow on the view screen. What a time to think about roasting marshmallows and hotdogs!

The computer increases the spin of the outer shell and the temperature decreases. We see a red-orange hue.

The Ark slows to 1,600 miles per hour as we reach an altitude of 200-miles above ground. The ride has been tame so far. If there was anyone on the ground that was able to hear us, we must have made a terrific sonic boom during this entry. The computer increases the spin of the outer shell and The Ark slows down quickly. We see a haze of blue, green and white on the view screen.

Now that the fireball has ended, the fiber optics clear up, and we can see green terrain coming up fast. The computer tells us our speed is now 200 miles per hour. The spin increases more, and we appear to stop within a foot of the ground. Everything seems so calm, pleasant and peaceful.

We get a surprise, when, without warning from the master computer, the spinning stops, and we drop like a four-mile wide rock. We feel the jolt! All the systems continue to work. The computer announces clearly "TOUCHDOWN!"

Each of us walks out of our pod and start looking at the data coming in about our surroundings. The air outside matches exactly the oxygen content of earth and all the other measurements are within the same specifications. We are feeling better about leaving The Ark and exploring our our new world.

We gather in the center of The Ark to review the information, discuss all our options and plan our next move. It looks like we found another Earth. Each of us takes time to give thanks in our own way for our safe journey here.

We vote to name our new location and planet and agree on the name Centauri Prime for our new city. Other cities will expand from ours, but everyone, including our descendants, will remember this was the first site. We will call our planet Centauria since we are in the Alpha section of the galaxy.

It has been six months now, and we have been exploring, cultivating and discovering things about our new planet wherever we go. It is amazing how easy it has been for each of us to adapt to our new home.

With the perfect timing expectant mothers seem to have; my precious granddaughter goes into labor. We are about to have our first citizen born.

In our medical department, I perform the delivery procedure, as I have done on each of the births before, and she delivers a baby boy. We can tell while I am cleaning him that he has good lungs. We will be able to hear him from a long distance. He is letting us know that he wants his mother!

We have another big celebration!

A month after the birth, we call a meeting to discuss our mission. We acknowledge that this journey has been free from any major arguments and we have worked in harmony to make this mission succeed. We made fantastic scientific discoveries and know that we can accomplish great things by working together.

We have accomplished the primary aspect of colonizing this planet since each family has had babies born that will carry on future generations. We have reached a pinnacle of civilization.

Four separate representatives of different nations have become one united group. We agree to sign a pact between each person, which, in the future beyond our lifetime, our descendants will pledge to follow. Our Unified World Covenant commands all citizens to, *"Do no harm to others"* and *"Help others when they are in need."* We have now conquered war.

With everyone in this mission working together, we have done away with the need for money, wealth and personal status. We have voted before every major decision for our community.

We have discussed and compromised when necessary, and been tolerant of every opinion given by each member. Each of us, with different cultures and beliefs, has been able to work together. We have now become a new civilized nation of individuals.

As our population grows and our descendants begin their communities, we want them to live in peace with those around them. We can only hope that future nations will get live together harmoniously and live by our covenants.

We will succeed and populate this new planet, Centauria, with our descendants. The future inhabitants of this planet will know that this new world started in our hometown, Centauri Prime.

Dedications

I would like to acknowledge the people who have been a part of my life during my first 50 years. Each has a special place in my heart and I pray for them every day. Thank you for everything you have done for me during my lifetime.

Carl Hixon: Pastor of Cedar Creek Missionary Baptist Church, Springfield, Arkansas. You taught me the Bible while you lead the church and helped me maintain my direction and purpose after I left home. I owe you more than you will ever know. I did not become a Chaplain's Assistant in the Air Force, but I used the wisdom I gained through you to be the best medic and nurse so that I could help others.

Quentin Vaughn: Technical Sergeant, USAF, Wilford Hall Medical Center, Ward A5, 1970. You were like a father to me, only better. You will never know how much it meant to hear you say, "That's nine level thinking." I became the best medic, trainer and nurse because I learned from the best. Thank you for the short time we worked together.

Jack Reed: You were a family friend of my Dad, but I always enjoyed the times you visited when I was growing up. You were the first man I ever heard tell my Dad to shut up and listen to what I had to say. I was going to name my first son after you, but it did not turn out that way. You always laughed when I told how he almost got his first name. I will always remember your white hair, friendly smile and firm handshake. Thank you for being there when I needed help.

Jim Grimshaw: Master Sergeant, USAF, Goosebay, Newfoundland, Labrador, Canada, 1975-1976. The first Master Sergeants I met who liked mopping and buffing floors over doing paperwork. Your guidance prepared me for the greatest assignment to end my career on. I loved every minute of my assignment at Goosebay because you and the other team members made me feel like I was part of the family. Thank you for being my friend and all the laughs we had while cleaning every Friday.

Gloria Evans, RN: Civilian Primary Care Clinic Nurse, USAF Hospital, Little Rock AFB, Arkansas, 1976-1978. You were my inspiration and model for being the best nurse, manager and leader I could be. I appreciated your help in maintaining the best clinic in the hospital. It would not have been as good or fun without you. I have tried my best to live your example by helping others in need. I owe you so much.

Dr. William S. Browner: Major, USAF, Elmendorf AFB, Anchorage, Alaska, 1978-1982. I have always admired your calm and caring treatment of patients. You accepted me for who I was and the skills I had to help others.

Dr. Jane Curtis: Captain, USAF, USAF Clinic Vance AFB, Enid, Oklahoma, 1987-1989. Thank you for believing in me and helping me become the best that I could be. Your efforts and encouragement in putting together the Minor Surgery Clinic helped me through the challenges thrown at me. Both of us left that clinic a better place than when we arrived. I never let the turkeys get me down.

John McReynolds: Colonel, U.S. Army National Guard, Enid, Oklahoma. It was a great pleasure to meet an officer of your caliber during my career. A leader is a man who can lead others without using his rank. You are truly an officer and a gentleman.

Andrea Vivia: Airman, USAF, Lackland AFB, Texas, 1971. You where the only patient to request me as your responding medic. You helped me understand that I have a gift for working with others in need. I believe I accomplished a lot for being a kid just off the farm. I hope your life has been just as fulfilling. Thank you for your dedication and service to our country.

The Airmen of 3701 Basic Military Training Squadron, Flight 1898, Lackland AFB, Texas. We started together on a cold winter night on December 8, 1969. Let's get together for a reunion.

Aimar, Dan L.; Alverson, Dennis K.; Bailey, Joel M.; Bernstein, David S.; Best, Jimmie E.; Best, Johnnie E.; Boughton, David W.; Brauning, John P. IV; Caslow, Steven G.; Chandler, Clyde D.; Clark, Randall S.; Crabtree, Jack R.; Dellipoala, Sam P.; Emery, Delmar G.; Faulk, Charles Jr.; Goff, Alan R.; Gottfried, Amos M.; Greer, Ronald L.; Hall, Leslie S.; Jackson, Jonny D.; Kight, Stephan R.; Kuehnl, Brian L.; Lockett, Henry; Lomp, Charles T.; Lowe, Billy T.; McCave, John E. Jr.; Morton, Roger W.; Neagle, David A.; Nopp, Nicholas H.; Parker, Clifford R.; Samuelson, Leonard J.; Sorrell, John H. Jr.; Spurlin, Russell L.; Whitmore, Ronald E.

Training Instructors: Technical Sergeant Wells and Sergeant Ira Parker.

Bill Sicard: Saint Paul Park, Minnesota Firefighter. Your spirit and dedication to help others showed Oklahoma and the world what caring and compassion means. We will always remember you.

Haywood and Ruth (Fryman) Gardner: Without them, this book would not be possible.

Dr. Susan Smith-Nash: University of Oklahoma, Humanities, 2000. If I had known humanities was going to be this much fun, I would have taken it first. You inspired me to write and this book is the completion of another part of my life. Thank you for your help and support.

Dr. Sidney Brown: Professor Emeritus, University of Oklahoma, Study of Jazz in Japan, 2000. Thank you for showing me the many sides of jazz. It was a wonderful class and you made it come alive with your own recollections.

Dr. Joe Whitecotton: Professor Emeritus, University of Oklahoma, Study of Jazz and music, 2000. This was a very different class than what I anticipated. Listening to music during class and at the bookstore was different and enjoyable. You made the music come alive.

Dr. Jane Bowerman: University of Oklahoma, Inter-Area Study, 2001. You brought everything together that I learned during my studies. Now, I put it all together in this book. Thank you for allowing me to let my imagination go free. Chapter Eight is dedicated to you.

Special Dedication

I want to extend a special dedication to everyone who is serving or has served in all our braches of military service in the United Sates. Thank you for all your hard work, leadership and the sacrifices you have made.

This country has the best military force in the world that is second to none. Many times in the history of this nation, you have been called to serve, and have won every war. Continue the great work and traditions.

I also want to recognize those who have made the ultimate sacrifice for our country and gave their life to protect and defend all of our freedoms we enjoy today as Americans.

www.ingramcontent.com/pod-product-compliance
Lightning Source LLC
Chambersburg PA
CBHW022002160426
43197CB00007B/232